Letting Go . . .

By Jodi Peppard-Latocki

Letting Go . . .
By Jodi Peppard-Latocki
Published by Jodi Peppard-Latocki
© 2020 Jodi Peppard-Latocki

ISBN #978-0-578-80910-6

This book is dedicated to my three biggest fans.

Thank You, Jesus, for taking my hand, day after day, and never, ever giving up on me. I look forward to one day breakdancing with You in Heaven, but in the meantime, I will enjoy this beautiful adventure with You here on earth!

My Joemama, thank you for being my best friend, husband, boyfriend, comedian, and adventure partner. I love growing in our faith together, encouraging one another daily and doing life with you!

Sofia Grace, my Boo, and my baby girl, thank you for always bringing God's joy, humor, and inspiration. Your life, since day one, drew me to the love and grace of Jesus. I am forever grateful! I love you so much, my beautiful daughter!

CONTENTS

Introduction   6

1. Letting Go   10

2. Tell Me Something Good   18

3. Not on My Watch   29

4. That's My Jam   40

5. Stinky Warrior   51

6. See You Tomorrow   65

7. Be Still   81

8. New   96

Conclusion   111

Acknowledgments   113

INTRODUCTION

Thank you for joining me in this letting-go journey. If you are here, it is for a reason. You've either found yourself in a season of having to let go of something, someone, or a situation. Or maybe you are just wanting to fire up and recharge your faith. Or maybe you just found this book and you're bored, so you've decided to read it. Either way, I am glad you are here.

God began to download the details of this devotional into my heart for a special reason and in an interesting season. I believe He will have empowering words to speak to you as well as you go through the pages of this book and confront areas in your life that you need to let go. I'm not going to lie to you and say this letting-go thing is easy, because it's not. That's why I wrote this devotional: to go through it with you and to remind you, you're not alone. It's a book + devotional + journal, which you can do on your own or with your small group or with a friend; you can even use it as curriculum in ministry. However, either way, I'm coming along with you for the ride. And it will be wild, but it's worth it.

Letting go is tough. Emotional, difficult, yet rewarding and freeing. It's like having a sliver in your index finger; it hurts like a mother in labor (well, maybe not entirely) while someone is probing, stabbing, and trying to get it out, but once it's out . . . Hallelujah! It feels oh so good and freeing! Plus, the results of letting go will leave you awestruck, transformed, and amazed at His goodness—much better than the outcome of a sliver removal, but you get the gist.

The Bible reminds us in Ecclesiastes 3 that there is a time for everything; we go through various seasons in life, and those seasons will include letting go, but with each season, there is always an exchange. An exchange that includes transformation, a new revelation, and freedom found in Him.

However, before you get started in this adventure, here is a little bit about my backstory . . . I grew up in a Christian home as a pastor's kid. (Don't judge me quite yet.) I encountered the presence of Jesus in my childhood, but I also saw the realities of real-life issues in full effect. As I stepped into my teenage years, I began to waver, questioning my faith and doubting my beliefs. I took my eyes off Jesus and refocused them on people and found myself judging and contemplating my faith in comparison to theirs. I faced trials that caused me to become skeptical: the trauma of almost losing my dad to a masked gunman who broke into our home with the intent to kill, causing PTSD for years to come; health issues that left me discouraged and distracted along with an array of other circumstances that vied for my attention and won. I was a hot mess, to say the least. These encounters caused a domino effect in my life that took me into a dark, lonely, and selfish place, which is altogether another story for another time.

Once I reached my early twenties, I found myself at the lowest point in life: in an abusive relationship but alone, pregnant, completely lost, and feeling hopeless. I felt as though I had searched here and there for happiness, success, and fulfillment, but continually came up short and unsatisfied. It was in that lonely and uncertain season that I began to count the cost of stepping into a relationship with Jesus again.

I remember praying a simple and somewhat hesitant prayer to Him, as if I were setting the parameters for the relationship: "Jesus, if I am going to do this life with You, I want the real deal, okay?!"—as if He would give us anything less—"I give my life to You, I want to start over, let's do this thing—together!" I felt His whisper reassuring my heart, "I've been waiting for you! Let's do this—together!" That is when my faith journey began and the truth about the letting-go process became a reality in my life.

My faith steps were as tiny as mustard seeds back then (if not tinier), so letting go seemed awfully slow, painful, and difficult, but Jesus never let go of my hand and still hasn't. He never pulls, or tugs, or drags, like a mom or dad trying to get their kids through a busy grocery store on an overscheduled weeknight. He just patiently waits, encourages along the way, with loving reminders: "Let's do this—together."

As you begin this devotional, you may have already discovered, letting go is a nonnegotiable necessity in life and it is imperative to our faith journey with Him. That is why we find ourselves right here, in this moment. If we are not letting go, we're stuck. And stuck leaves us complacent and comfortable, yet miserable, lingering in our own mess. It prevents God from doing His thing in us, keeping us stagnant and unchanged.

So, as you begin this devotional, prepare your heart for what He's calling you to let go of. It may surprise you at first, frustrate you along the way, then leave you feeling free in the end. But the journey is worth it. I believe, as you begin letting go with His help, you will find your freedom in surrender.

CHAPTER 1

Letting Go

I stared at the four walls of the classroom I had been teaching in for thirteen years and sobbed. The place where I stepped out in crazy faith. At the time, I was a twenty-eight-year-old woman, feeling unsure of myself, insecure in my abilities, no experience, no special talent, no credentials, and no real plan besides relying on the dream and passion God had given me to step out in ministry.

The room was filled with sweet visions and special memories of decorating the walls for a new series that would make God's Word come alive. Times of my most sincere cries of desperation for God's help and prayers for kids to encounter His presence filled my thoughts. Fun nights filled with laughter, watching movies, eating snacks, and the smell of Cheetos and dirty feet (the true aroma that prove kids are having a blast) flooded my emotions.

Faces that grew up in that classroom, during their elementary years, raced through my mind like a movie reel as I ugly-cried harder. The joys of dancing and singing with the kids during our praise and worship time, as we would shout as loud as possible with the ultimate goal of their parents hearing us in the sanctuary.

The lightbulb moments of revelation as God's Word came alive in the hearts of each child, while hearing God's personal message to each one of us, kids, and leaders alike.

The place where I knew I had nothing to give but just my plain ole self and God seemed completely okay with that. The position where I discovered my God-given gifts as I quit comparing myself with other pastors and just became an audience of *One*. I sat on the floor, eyes swollen, and I began to question my next crazy faith steps . . . to leave it all behind.

To say good-bye to the comforts of where I found myself and my calling, the safety of knowing my day-to-day plans and activities. The place where I found my identity and purpose in life. To not seeing my best friends anymore or being involved in the daily life of my church family. To let it all go.

I am learning in this faith journey that we will always face letting-go moments. These moments can be painful, uncomfortable, difficult, and emotional, but letting go is necessary when we do life with Him. In fact, letting go is a part of our adventure with Him. It is a call to obey, requiring a new level of trust in Him for the next part of our journey. Letting go means surrender; it's giving Him full control of the wheel while we raise our hands in exhilaration (in the passenger seat and most often feeling blindfolded), taking a deep breath in, with our bellies full of butterflies, while He leads us into His extraordinary expedition.

I am discovering more recently—very slowly and, at moments, hesitantly—that the only way I can *truly* let go and step into His *all-knowing* plan is to understand fully who I really am—in Him. That is where I find myself now. How about you? It's going to be a risk, I know, and at times it feels like we're losing it all, but it's what He's calling us to: fully trusting Him as we let go and allow Him to redefine us and lead us into the unknown.

In Genesis 12, Abraham had to let go. The Lord told him, leave your land, leave your people, leave what's comfortable, leave what you had, leave the familiar, leave the memories, leave your day-to-day plans, just leave and let it go because there's something else I have for you. Abraham didn't know the next steps or the next item on the yellow legal notepad of things to cross off. He just surrendered, obeyed, left, let go, and moved on, just as God told him to do. I'm nowhere as cool and courageous as Abraham was or as mature in the faith, by any means, but one thing I've come to understand, like Abraham, is when God says to let go, it's best to do just that . . . let go.

God never promises that it will be easy or comfortable or without emotion, but He does promise that He will never leave us or forsake us; He will never let go of our hand in the journey of letting go. In fact, Philippians 1:6 (AMP) reminds us, "I am convinced *and* confident of this very thing, that He who has begun a good work in you will [continue to] perfect *and* complete it until the day of Christ Jesus [the time of His return]."

This letting-go thing may feel uncomfortable and uncertain when the next step looks foggy, but if He calls us to it, we can be certain, He will not stop there. Are you in a place, like me, having to let go? Maybe you are in a similar situation, where He is calling you to let go of something or someone or a situation. It may be something familiar or something you have held onto for so long that it's a part of who you are now; maybe it's someone who broke your heart or let you down. It could be a situation that conflicts with your faith and challenges your beliefs. It might be baggage that keeps piling up or comfort that halts your next steps, an idea that you cling to or a perspective that enslaves you. It could be a feeling of anger, hatred, insecurity, or fear. If He's calling you to let go, you can rest in the promise of knowing this: He's a completer of what He's started, and He has something else just for you, something new as you let go.

So, what do you say? Are you willing to join me on this wild ride of trusting Him and letting go? I promise to hold your hand tightly through the unknowns and scream at the top of my lungs with you through the process! Plus, I want to encourage you to journal along the ride! You won't want to miss or forget

a word, vision, dream, idea, thought, or encouragement that He has just for you,

as you are letting go.

Reflection Questions:

What are some things God is calling you to let go of? Ask Him, He will tell you.

It can be good or bad, comforts or insecurities, passions or lies, people or

situations, bad habits or plans, etc. As you write them down, tell God that you are

committed to letting go.

_____

_____

_____

_____

_____

_____

_____

_____

_____

_____

_____

_____

Don't worry, He will begin to reveal the "why" behind the reason you need to let go as you walk through these pages.

Write down what He is showing you now as you begin this journey with Him.

_____

_____

_____

_____

_____

_____

_____

_____

_____

_____

_____

_____

_____

_____

Be encouraged: He has begun a good work in you, and He promises, and pinky swears to complete it, even though you can't fully see it all right now while you're letting go.

CHAPTER 2

Tell Me Something Good

2020 has been a year to remember—a year of loss, sadness, sickness, and disappointments. Letdowns and sorrows. Plans ruined and wrecked, dreams cut short with ever-changing rules and regulations. Memes and sarcasm. Politics, uncertainties, hatred in the media, injustice, and disarray—while we are all waiting patiently (well, maybe more passive-aggressively now) for some good news to arrive.

I would find myself in the early months of quarantine seeking out any good news I could find on social media, the local news, world news, YouTube, and anywhere else there might be a smidgen of hope, something to brighten my day, so maybe, just maybe, I could brighten someone else's. As the months went on and the world seemed to worsen, I could feel my soul cry out, "TELL ME SOMETHING GOOD!!" Over time, I found myself having to let go of news sources, certain social media platforms, and muting all things infecting my heart with negativity. I began to dive more intentionally into the Word of God with the desperation and cry of "Lord, please tell me something good. I need *your* encouragement and *your* truth." My heart ached. The heaviness was exhausting. And my perspective needed refreshing.

At 4:00 a.m. one morning, I woke up after a crazy, uncanny, and wild dream. I knew it had a spiritual context to it, but I could not quite grasp why or what it meant. I did not wake up feeling fear, anger, or guilt; in fact, I woke with the sense that it was about me accomplishing what I was called to do. Foggy brained and baffled, I sipped my hot coffee and pondered my dream.

In my dream, I was binding an evil man with heavy rope around his ankles and hands. (Side note: I am not a bully or a fighter, I'm not even athletic, I can hardly throw a frisbee, so the idea of me capturing someone and binding them with rope is unheard of and would be miraculous and possibly a hilarious sight to all who know me!) As I was binding him, I felt no anger or fear or guilt, as I said before; I just felt certainty that I was called to do this job and I was accomplishing what I was called to do. This man began to spew nasty, demeaning, belittling, disgusting comments at me; however, I gave him no attention and I continued my capture while I called for someone to hand me the duct tape to put over his mouth.

I knew his words were filth, but I have no recollection of what his words actually were because it was as if I gave them no attention or power to penetrate my heart, my soul, my feelings, or my thoughts. His words had nothing on me. I knew I had authority over him. I knew I was doing what I was called to do; I had the physical strength to bind him with the mental toughness to disregard his sneers and insults. As I journaled and spent time praying to God, I continued to be perplexed about what this dream meant.

Two days later, while worshipping, I sang along to "Do It Again," a song by Elevation Worship. I sensed the Lord revealing to me the interpretation of my dream. He reminded me, as His children we have the keys to His Kingdom. We have His authority! He continued to bring to light the fact that I was binding the enemy in my dream—a job that He gave us to do.

The word *binding* is not a regular word in my daily vocabulary. I just assumed it meant (according to my "Jodi dictionary") "tying up with rope." So, I decided to look it up with good ole Google and here's what I found at YourDictionary.com. The definition of binding used as an adjective is "something that limits or holds someone to an agreement."[1]

God began to take me to various verses in His Word about binding. I found myself in Matthew 16. If you read the entire paragraph of Matthew 16:13–20, you can see that Jesus is giving His amazing, miraculous, powerful, love-inspired authority to His followers. Ahem . . . that means *you* and *me*! This is just one of the many rad perks we have as God's kids.

The part that truly stood out the most to me was Matthew 16:19 (AMP) in the Jesus rock-star red letters: "And I will give you the keys (authority) of the kingdom of heaven; and whatever you bind [forbid, declare to be improper and unlawful] on earth will have [already] been bound in heaven, and whatever you loose [permit, declare lawful] on earth will have [already] been loosed in heaven."

I began to weep as I read this. I needed to hear this. I needed to know this truth, and I needed to hear this good news. It was a week of letting go. I was releasing special people in my life to God, fully trusting them to Him. It was emotional and challenging because I sensed a loss of who I was as I surrendered them to Him.

To let go of our control and to give Him *all* control is uncomfortable. But it's as if God knew I needed Him, in that moment, to interrupt my sleep and download a version of me I had not seen or believed existed. A strong image of myself that only He had. A reflection of a justice-minded and powerful Captain Marvel character, in the spiritual realm, taking care of business, squashing evil and probably really good at throwing a frisbee. It reminded me of how good God is at showing up in our most vulnerable, lonely, weak, and uncertain moments and giving us His perspective of who we really are—in Him.

Remember when Gideon hid in fear while threshing wheat at the bottom of a winepress to hide the grain from the mean Midianites who'd been wreaking havoc on his people, the Israelites; when all along the job was supposed to be done outside in the open air?! Judges 6:12 (NLT) says, "The angel of the LORD appeared to him and said, 'Mighty hero, the LORD is with you!'" Gideon was not mighty. He probably threw a frisbee just like I do. He was hiding in fear, doing a job *inside* that was meant to be done *outside*. He was not living in faith. He knew he was a wimp; he knew his clan was the weakest link, and he knew he was the least important in his family. In fact, everyone knew that. Yet God saw him through His lens and considered him a "mighty hero." God reminded him in verse 14 (ERV), "The LORD turned toward Gideon and said, 'Then use your great power and go save the Israelites from the Midianites. I am sending you to save them.'" There goes God *giving*, while you, Gideon, and I must *let go*.

If you are needing some good news, well, I have some. God sees you. However, not as you see yourself. You and I have been given God's authority, just like Gideon. To bind not only the enemy but all that he stands for. His lies, the fears, the doubts, the depression, the insecurities, the uncertainties, the sickness, the disease, and all the garbage we find ourselves believing in, wallowing around in, and accepting as our normal. As we bind this garbage here on earth, we can loosen what heaven has already declared as ours.

We are God's kids. What's His is ours. He's given us the key. *His* key of authority. The same power that raised Jesus from the dead lives in you and me! We can walk with confidence knowing *whom* we belong to, *who* we are in Him, and *where* our strength and authority come from. Isn't that *good news*?!

Well, if your soul has been screaming out just like mine, "TELL ME SOMETHING GOOD!!" . . . here it is! Blast some worship jams, raise your hands, get ready to dance and sing your heart out! He wants to fill you up. He already knows your fragile state, your emotional instability, and even your frisbee-throwing skills. He is already aware of how you see yourself. However, He wants to fill your soul with His truth about you—your identity, your dreams, your emotions, and your thoughts. He has something *good* for you right now and in every season you may find yourself in.

Reflection Questions:

How do you honestly *see* yourself? You can be raw and real, trust me with this.

_____

_____

_____

_____

_____

_____

_____

_____

_____

_____

How do you believe God *sees* you? If you are not sure of His view, ask Him and

check out what His Word has to say about you. Research, study, and find out!

_____

_____

_____

_____

_____

_____

_____

_____

_____

_____

_____

How do your views differ from God's view of you?

_____

_____

_____

_____

_____

_____

_____

_____

_____

_____

_____

_____

What idea or view of yourself do you need to bind (forbid, declare to be improper and unlawful) because it has been holding you captive and keeping you from His purpose?

_____

_____

_____

_____

_____

_____

_____

_____

_____

_____

_____

_____

_____

_____

What God truths do you need to loosen from heaven over your identity? As you

write them down, make them personal. Start each one with "I am"!

_____

_____

_____

_____

_____

_____

_____

_____

_____

_____

_____

_____

As you write these things down, take time to worship Him and enjoy His

presence. He has valuable, precious, and oh-so-*good* things to download to you

and about you.

CHAPTER 3

Not on My Watch

I grew up as the middle sister in my family among three siblings. If you have any siblings, you know firsthand the hilarity and craziness of a sibling relationship and all that comes along with it: rivalry, name-calling, wrestling matches, hair pulling, tattling, sleepovers, pretending, stealing one another's things, pranks, fights, screaming matches, and the straight-up dysfunctional, live, raw reality of a love-hate, priceless relationship between siblings. Or was this just my family?! Well, even if it was just my family, I would not trade it for anything. My siblings were my best friends whom I made fun of, laughed with, yelled at, got in trouble with, stole from, screamed at, and said I love you to—all in a twenty-four-hour period! Talk about crazy town—but I loved every second of it.

As I grew up and found myself in my teenage years, I began to recognize the labels people placed on my siblings and me as children, labels of comparison, labels of lacking, and labels of less than. Labels that represented people's opinions of me and views based on their personal perspectives. I began to attach these labels, valid or not, to myself as I tried to figure out my worth in the world. Statements I adopted as my truth and my identity; I wore them like a name badge identifying who I was to anyone who met me. "Hello, my name is Jodi. I am not that pretty, but that's okay—I'm funny. I am sensitive and thoughtful, but I'm afraid of everything, insecure, and not sure of my worth. I'm not as artsy and beautiful as Leah, or as athletic and popular as Greg, or as pretty and independent as Jen, but this is me. This is who I am."

As I became an adult and then a pastor, working with children, I began to see this labeling firsthand. Labels given to children by a teacher, a bully, a friend, a family member, a coach, a complete stranger in a grocery store. Declarations that declare: not special, not good enough, not strong enough, unable, cannot, and won't. Seeing the stronghold of these labels on others stirred in me a desire to confront the labels that were spoken over my life with God's Word.

The devil loves labels because they allow him to distort, manipulate, and twist the true identity of our being. Labels we put on ourselves and labels people put on us limit us from God's potential. Labels from our childhood can keep us from the purpose Christ has for us. Labels that halt, paralyze, and discourage can cause doubts and hopelessness. These labels lie, steal, kill, and destroy the God-size dreams in our hearts and remind us of who we are not and who we will never be.

I was recently going through some random items as I was trying to declutter my house. I came across a teacup and a saucer. I thought about throwing it out or donating it along with my other seemingly undervalued items I did not need any longer. This teacup looked worthless to me. It had nothing that screamed special, valuable, or important. It wasn't something I used or felt I needed. I could not understand why I would have held onto it for this long, especially if it did not hold some kind of value.

I racked my brain, trying to figure out where the teacup came from and why it was just tucked away with other irrelevant items in my storage space. I decided not to trust my perspective alone, so I googled the label I found on the bottom of the saucer. I ended up discovering that this teacup and saucer was a rare antique collector's item that was selling for over two hundred dollars on eBay. What I had planned to toss out or donate, what seemed worthless in my eyes, had incredible value for its smallness and meaningless stature. Its value came from its creator, Aynsley England, one of the oldest ceramic firms in London.

As I spend time with God (you know, the Creator of the universe we find in Genesis 1, the One who created the heavens and the earth as well as you and me!), I'm reminded that the only *One* who can truly and honestly label us is the *One* who created us. The Creator of humankind provides the value to His creation: the meaning, the worth, the authenticity, the purpose, the genuineness. His view of us outweighs anyone's opinion, idea, or perspective, any day and all day long. The question is, whose view do you believe?

I have had two dreams about snakes in my entire lifetime. I hate snakes, for obvious reasons. But it just so happens that the two dreams I had about snakes were exactly two weeks apart from one another, both on a Monday night, in a season of confronting my own labels using the Word of God.

The first dream took place at a pool. I was staring in the pool and saw something in it. I could not quite make it out, but while staring intensely to figure it out, I ended up falling in the pool. As the image drew clearer, I began to see that I was staring at a long snake swimming, or slithering, in the pool. The pool was quite large, so the threat of the snake seemed less concerning as long as it did not see me or get near me. I swam to the other side rather quickly, deep water and all, so I could get out before it reached me. As I went to jump out, I felt the presence of something behind me. I turned to look, and it was the snake coming closer to me. The snake knew I was there, and it was watching me.

I tried to yell for my husband, Joe, to pray for me, because I could see him in the distance, but I could not get his attention or make a sound; nothing came out. The words formed from my mouth, but as the air released from my lips, it was more remote than a whisper. I remember wanting to quote the Word of God

from Mark 16:17–18—about snake venom not hurting me or something like

that?!—but I didn't know the verse well enough even to believe what it had to

say. It's interesting to think that I knew prayer and God's Word was my weapon

in this dream and I knew I needed it desperately to survive the fear I had.

I woke up immediately, in the middle of the night, sweating profusely,

holding my breath in fear and terror. I began to take slow, deep breaths as I

prayed myself back to sleep. The next morning, I wrote this dream down, while I

read and masterly memorized Mark 16:17–18.

Two weeks later I had the next snake dream; this time, I was in my front

yard. A long, large snake, much bigger than the first one, slithered around my

feet, slowly and surely trying to get a grip on me. It swirled around me in a slow

devious figure-eight rotation. It seemed interested in biting me; however, I began

to squeeze it back with my feet, as if to let it know, "I can do the same thing back

to you, buster." We communicated through our actions and knowing that it was

planning to take me out, I was not having it.

I seemed to be strong enough to squeeze this ginormous python wrapped

tightly around my appendages, with my 8.5-size woman feet. I became

empowered as words began to fly out of my mouth; I spoke with command as I squeezed back with my feet: "You have no authority over me. You have no right! I belong to Jesus Christ! You cannot win. I have you under *my* feet! Leave me alone in Jesus's name!"

With every word and every squeeze, I grew stronger in my strength and in my faith. The snake was now trying to get away from me, and any ounce of fear I did have was now gone. I released the snake from my clutches, and it slithered away quickly, as if to say, "I'm done with you." I began to take a few steps forward to walk away, but I sensed a sneak attack from behind.

Just as I turned to look, it was back, in full-fledged attack mode around my feet. So again, I stepped on it. I wasn't sure if it bit me this time or not, but I really didn't care because I knew the scriptures. (Venom ain't got nothing on me!) I began to speak God's Word *out loud* to let the snake know I knew *the truth* and it was time for this thing to leave. It was not allowed to bother me any longer, not on my watch.

When I woke up, I wrote the dream down and told Joe all about it. About an hour later Joe texted me Luke 10:18–20 (ERV), "Jesus said to them, 'I saw Satan falling like lightning from the sky. He is the enemy, but know that I have given you more power than he has. I have given you power to crush his snakes and scorpions under your feet. Nothing will hurt you. Yes, even the spirits obey you. And you can be happy, not because you have this power, but because your names are written in heaven.'" Did you hear that?! Jesus has given you more power than the enemy has; in fact, you were created to crush him (his lies and his labels) under your feet. And seriously, what label can compete with the fact that *your name* is written in *heaven*?! Pause and think about that for a few minutes!

It's time for a serious heart check. Are you tired of the labels you've attached yourself to—labels given to you as a kid or ones you've given to yourself? The ones the enemy tries to manipulate you with? The lies he uses to sneak attack when you're not looking? Which ones are you holding onto that do not line up with what your Creator says about you? Look at what God's Word says specifically about *you*. Read His thoughts about you *out loud* to yourself and over yourself (in your Morgan Freeman voice if need be). Make them personal so they infiltrate your heart, your thoughts, and your soul—until you believe *the truth* about who you really are.

You are God's kid. You are His precious child (John 1:12). God calls *you* His friend (John 15:15). God specifically chose *you*—even when you feel like you're the last pick at everything in life, He chose *you* first (Eph. 1:3–8). You can do *all* things through Christ who gives you strength (Phil. 4:13). You can boast about your weaknesses, because it's only when you're weak, that everything can be done completely by God's power (not yours!), so when you are weak, you are *actually* strong in Him (2 Cor. 12:9–10). You are sealed by the Holy Spirit, God's Spirit. *His Spirit resides in you.* Jesus has saved you and identified you as His very own; His seal is on your life! When the enemy looks at you, he sees *whom* you belong to (Eph. 1:13).

Nehemiah 8:10 reminds us—the joy that you receive from God is your ultimate strength. His joy in you is unlike anything else—it is something that cannot be stolen or contended for. The definition of who *you* are, according to your Creator—the identity and worth He's placed in you and on you—stretches across the pages of His Word.

You are forgiven (Col. 1:13–14). *You* are complete in Him (Col. 2:9–10). *You* have direct access to Him (Heb. 4:14–16). *You* are unconditionally, extravagantly loved by Him (1 John 3:1). *You* cannot be separated from His unstoppable love for you, no matter what you think, say, believe, or do (Rom. 8:31–39). *You* are His priceless masterpiece (Eph. 2:10). Not only has He given you His power and His authority; you can also be filled with His unspeakable joy and happiness, because your name (Yes, *yours*!) is written in the journals of heaven (Luke 10:18–20).

Your identity in Him has *everything* to do with your destiny with Him. Page after page, word after word in His Word, is His love letter to *you* and His love story about *you*. So, what labels, lies, and straight-up trash have you been believing about yourself that you need to say . . . not on my watch.

Reflection Questions:

This may be difficult to rehash, but it is important, nonetheless. Take a moment to write down the labels spoken over you throughout your life. These labels may come from people you love, strangers, or acquaintances you hardly know, or even your own beliefs about yourself. After you write all these labels down, I dare you to find a verse for each one, in God's Word, from your Creator, that says otherwise. Write the verse directly next to the label you have attached yourself to, which the Word of God defies. As you stare at each label you have believed for so long, compare it now to the truth of your Creator. Ask yourself, which one are you going to believe from this moment on?

Labels: Verses:

_____   _____

_____   _____

_____   _____

_____   _____

_____   _____

_____   _____

_____   _____

_____   _____

_____   _____

_____   _____

_____   _____

_____   _____

_____   _____

James 1:6 (NLT) says, "But when you ask him, be sure that your faith is in God alone. Do not waver, for a person with divided loyalty is as unsettled as a wave of the sea that is blown and tossed by the wind." This is your time to trust Him alone. Not to waver between believing the labels placed on you and what God has to say about you. It is your opportunity to choose, to stop being unsettled in your mind and emotions, and to receive His truth about you. Are you willing to believe what God says about *you*? As you process your decision (and it's okay to take your time with this), take a black permanent marker and cross off the statement you refuse to believe any longer. As you do, you can say . . . not on my watch.

CHAPTER 4

That's My Jam

I find myself overplaying my favorite songs over and over and over again. Do you do that too? Or am I just weird? "That's MY JAM!" I'll shout out, even though my family gets annoyed by the one-hundredth replay in a row, because I'm driving and I get full control of what song comes on next, with the volume at full blast as my endorphins run high.

During this season of letting go, I find myself not only replaying my favorite songs but also replaying all of my decisions—the choices I've made, the steps that I've taken, the path that I've followed—everything that has led me straight to where I am, in this very moment, right now. Letting go is already a very lonely experience, but when you begin to replay your life's journey out in your mind, there's a sense of wondering, "What am I doing, where am I going, and am I losing who I am?" in this God process of letting go.

You know when it's 4:00 a.m. and you cannot sleep, it really hits you to the core: you are committed now, no turning back, but you feel stuck in the waiting. Your trust in God doesn't seem to be as strong in these late-night, early-morning moments, and you begin debating the losses in your mind that make you want to crawl back to everything that was comfortable and easy. Every single thing that made you feel safe and stable, whether it was dysfunctional or not. The tears flow swiftly, and it is hard to keep from waking the whole house up with your sobbing and sniffling and snot blowing.

This is the time and the crucial moment when my faith in Him is truly challenged. It is in these moments, when the sun hasn't quite risen yet (literally or figuratively), that I find myself having to cling to His Word. Turning *every* promise, *every* revelation, and *every* period at the end of each sentence into my statement, my truth, *my jam*. Replaying it over and over and over again, not only for my endorphins to increase but for the sake of my sanity.

I must *choose* to take His hand, to believe and trust His Word over anything I feel, anything I see, anything I think, or anything I understand. This is where faith takes some serious action. "Faith is what makes real the things we hope for. It is proof of what we cannot see . . . Faith helps us understand that God created the whole world by his command. This means that the things we see were made by something that cannot be seen" (Heb. 11:1–3 ERV). And this *same* faith, which I am desperate for at this very moment, can only come from *one* source: His Word. My Jam.

"So faith comes from hearing the message, and the message that is heard is what Christ spoke" (Rom. 10:17 GW). The entire Word of God is our Truth. It is the lamp to our feet. The light to our path. It is living and active and sharper than any two-edged sword. It discerns the thoughts and intentions of our heart. It is breathed by God Almighty and useful for teaching and for showing us what is wrong in our lives. It corrects faults and teaches the right way to live. It exposes our issues. It reveals our pride. It's like an X-ray, revealing what's really going on inside us.

It is a priceless gift to be treasured. It brings healing—physically, emotionally, mentally, and spiritually. It makes us whole. As we hide it in our hearts, it keeps us from sin. The Word completes us and equips us for every good work. His Word does not return void; it harvests, and it brings results. It makes things happen that God calls to happen and succeeds at what God calls to succeed. Every Word of God proves *true*.

The Word of God became flesh and dwelt among us, died in our place, and rose from the dead—*defeating* death so that we may live. The Word gives us our strength, even at the lonely hour of 4:00 a.m. It is our foundation, our anchor, our resting place, and our rock. It never fails or falters. It is steady, true, and constant. In fact, Isaiah 55:8–9 spells it out so clearly and thankfully so, especially in seasons we do not understand. His thoughts are not like our thoughts. His ways are not like ours. His are higher, His are greater, and His are better. (Thank God!) This is why I need His Word, my jam, in these moments.

It is my solid ground and sanity as I find myself questioning all things and feeling as though I have lost everything. When uncertainty seems bigger than my faith and fear appears to be larger than my trust, when I am confronted to the core with all the letting go, His Word reminds me of who He is in the midst of me losing who I am. It's there, when I least expect it, in my pit of uncertainty, that I discover I'm in the exact place He wants me to be, recognizing all of Him as He redefines all of me and who He's calling me to be—through His Word.

Jesus Himself reminds us, "The whole world, earth and sky, will be destroyed, but my words will last forever" (Mark 13:31 ERV). His Word is our constant, unfailing, forever source of fulfillment, truth, and hope. So, have you found *your* jam yet, your word in His Word that can never be destroyed?

What are you clinging to at 4:00 a.m. when the world is asleep and bleak? When you are questioning everything about the season you find yourself in, second-guessing where you are or where you're going? You have sixty-six books to choose from, each full of tried-and-true jam sessions. When you know you can't rest on how you feel, or rely on what you think, or believe in what you see, His Word will lead you and guide you.

What revelation are you clinging to? What is He saying to you in this season of letting go? Philippians 4:6–7 (NLT) has been my tried-and-true jam in my season of letting go. My golden nugget that I am replaying for the zillionth time at full volume. "Don't worry about anything; instead, pray about everything. Tell God what you need and thank him for all he has done. Then you will experience God's peace, which exceeds anything we can understand. His peace will guard your hearts and minds as you live in Christ Jesus."

I encourage you to find yours—*your jam*. And when you do, replay it as many times as you need to, on *full blast*, with a proud stance, as you take ownership and yell out, "THAT'S MY JAM!"

Reflection Questions:

Open His Word wherever you feel led and just begin to read. As you spend time in His Word and presence, take time to listen and worship Him as you play the song "Take Courage" (a song by Bethel Music and Kristene DiMarco). Where do you find yourself in His Word?

_____

_____

_____

_____

Why did you choose that book? That chapter? That verse?

_____

_____

_____

_____

_____

_____

_____

_____

_____

_____

_____

_____

_____

Put yourself in the story or the scriptures you are reading. How is this relevant to you and your life right now?

_____

_____

_____

_____

_____

_____

_____

_____

_____

_____

_____

How do you relate with the story or the situation in the scriptures you landed on?

Engage your senses: what do you smell, hear, see, taste, or touch?

_____

_____

_____

_____

_____

_____

_____

_____

_____

_____

_____

_____

What words bring you comfort? Hope? Truth? Security? Joy? Strength? Explore why.

_____

_____

_____

_____

_____

_____

_____

_____

_____

_____

_____

_____

Where do you find yourself pausing and reflecting as you explore God's Word?

_____

_____

_____

_____

_____

_____

_____

_____

_____

_____

_____

What is His Word speaking to you, right now, in this season?

_____

_____

_____

_____

_____

_____

_____

_____

_____

_____

_____

_____

_____

Today, find your promise, your truth, and your *jam* in His Word and make it yours. Cling to it. It is for you. It is your faith builder and your foundation. It is the place where you will discover the peace that surpasses all that you see, feel, think, and understand. It is *your* tried-and-true jam session that will never fail or falter.

CHAPTER 5

Stinky Warrior

One of my most favorite movies of all time is *Nacho Libre.* It is one of those movies I can watch over and over and over again and still laugh so hard that I cry. If you have not seen it yet, you need to get on that today! It is hilarious and fun and has a great message; plus, with Jack Black acting as the main character, it wins all around.

I won't share too much, but the overall message of the film portrays Ignacio (Nacho), a cook at a monastery orphanage in Mexico, where he too grew up because his parents passed away when he was a baby. His greatest dream and desire is to become a *luchador* (fighter), but wrestling, or fighting of any kind, is completely forbidden by the monastery because it is considered a sin of vanity. Ignacio stinks at being a cook (which he hates doing anyway), but he also discovers that he stinks at fighting too (which is a bummer, because it's his dream). He loves all the orphans at the orphanage; he's committed to them and his oath to God, but he feels conflicted by the "why" behind his purpose and his dream.

In the rising action of the film, we find Nacho praying this prayer to God, "Precious Father, why have you given me this desire to wrestle and then made me such a stinky warrior?"[2] It is in that moment Nacho asks for a sign from God and God literally brings the straight-fire truth to Nacho, the understanding behind it all.

I guess I relate with Nacho all too well, at least during the rising action part. Maybe that's why I love this movie so much. I find myself comfortable in my stretchy pants, asking God about the desires that I have, but feeling like I stink at them and wondering about my purpose.

Last year God revealed a powerful truth to me about the desires of our hearts. It was a normal day for me, and I had plans to visit a friend of mine who had six-month-old twins at the time. Before heading over to her house that afternoon, I had plans to pick up my groceries from my local grocery store. As I jammed my favorite tunes and drove to the store for pickup, I began planning, in my head, to pick up a dozen bright orange flowers for my friend. She was at home a lot during this time with not just one but two baby boys, plus working part-time at home, while the Michigan winter was ever-so-slowly coming to an end.

I knew she needed a bright, happy, pick-me-up, and I knew these flowers would do just that. I was super excited to surprise her as I rolled into the parking lot. I decided to grab my grocery order first, and then I would check out the floral department for the special surprise I had planned.

I parked my car and called the number on the sign to let them know I had arrived. A few minutes later, I saw a man rolling a huge cart full of groceries toward my car. As he got closer, I noticed a beautiful bouquet of orange flowers sitting on top. Immediately, I got frustrated as the cart came closer to my car and I thought to myself, "What the heck?! They messed up my order *again*! They are giving me items I did not ask for. Ugh! Let's *also* see what they forgot from my list!"

As the man greeted me, I rolled my car window down with irritability tattooed across my face (I am sure of it). I waited for him to begin to go over the list of items they missed. Right away, he said, "Hi Jodi!" with a pleasant voice and kind attitude, while my WWJD upbringing was tucked under my car seat, along with the trash I'd hidden. I chimed right back, hoping not to snap my irritation toward him. "Hi! I think you might have the wrong cart for me. I didn't order that bouquet of flowers on top!" He responded kindly with, "Yes, I know. Our floral department is giving away bouquets today to our pickup customers. So, these are for you!"

He handed them to me, a beautiful, bright, lively bouquet of orange flowers, just as I imagined picking out for my friend that very day. I sank down in my car seat, embarrassed and undignified, and thanked the man for the super sweet gesture.

The flowers stared at me from my passenger seat the whole ride home while I felt silly and stupid at how I reacted in my heart and in my head about the item I wasn't supposed to get, nor did I deserve them with my bad attitude. I began to talk to God out loud about it as I teared up: "Thank You, Lord, for blessing me with this beautiful orange bouquet of flowers. They were *exactly* what I had envisioned for Rachel, but you knew that . . . didn't you?!" I began to chuckle as I cried, thinking about how cool God is (even when we act stupid) and how He gives us the desires of our hearts, without us even saying a word, just like Psalm 37:4 states.

As I continued to drive with tears flowing down my cheeks and a giggle in my heart, I felt like He was trying to get something else through to me. I could not shake the fact that for some crazy reason, on this very regular, normal, mundane Monday, He wanted me to understand something more about our desires. So I asked Him, "God, what else are you trying to show me?" He whispered gently to my heart, "Not only do I give you your heart's desires, but I am also the One who puts those desires in your heart in the first place."

I was speechless. I pulled into my driveway and began to cry tears of joy. Now maybe this is not news to you at all, but for me this whisper from God Almighty was revolutionary. This was some serious news that I needed desperately, like yesterday. I sat in my driveway, a jeep full of groceries and a bouquet of bright orange beautiful flowers winking at me with God's amazing mysterious way of paralyzing me with His wild and extravagant love. I did not ask another question; I just cried tears of gratitude.

That word He whispered to me that day still has me awestruck today. Why, you may ask? Because it is one thing that the God of the Universe *gives* His kids the desires of their hearts, but it is a whole other mind-blowing, fascinating thought that He *put* those desires there in the first place.

One morning recently, I was spending time with Him, listening to "Peace, Be Still," a song by Lauren Daigle from Bethel's Heaven Come 2018 tour. I closed my eyes tightly and just listened to the words. I had played this song a gazillion times before but just wanted to sit back and absorb every little bit of it.

Suddenly I began to envision myself in a boat. As I looked up, I could see Jesus exactly in front of me, about four to six feet away, His left hand held out toward me. He was standing on the water (like He owned it) while I sat comfortably in my boat. The water around Him was ferociously crashing. The waves could take over an oil tanker. The sky was dark, with high winds, and loud thunder shook the sky while the lightning flashed like fireworks on the Fourth of July. But for some crazy reason I had no fear.

My small boat was steady as a rock as I stared back at my best friend in the whole wide world. Now in reality, I have never been out in the middle of the ocean like this nor do I know how to swim, so the idea that I was fearless, in a small boat, in the middle of a raging sea, during a storm, was unbelievable. Yet I had certainty that I was safe. I made the decision to get out and walk toward Him.

I recognized immediately that Jesus was not making me get out of the boat or even willing to help me out of the boat. He stood four to six feet away intentionally, giving me the choice to meet Him where He was. There was no pressure, no shame, no guilt, not even a word, just a smile and a hand offering to take mine. I stepped out and walked toward Him. I was not even fazed by the fact I was walking on a wild sea that could swallow me up in a matter of seconds.

When I met Him where He was, I took His hand, and we began to slow dance together on the majestic and untamed sea. We laughed together, but mostly at me, because I had no idea how to dance with a partner; as He twirled me around, we laughed hysterically. All the while, the storm and the sea became the background stage and the sound effects surrounding our beautiful dance routine.

God reminded me once again about the dreams and desires He gives us. We can all find ourselves comfortable in a boat, holding tightly to our dreams, while feeling lost and defeated as we begin looking for our own way of making them a reality. He reminded me of His promise found in James 4:8 (ERV), "Come near to God, and He will come near to you . . ." He is a gentleman, so there is no shame, guilt, or push from Him. You can be as close to Him as you want to be—your choice. He graciously waits patiently as we decide to come near, to step out and take His hand or hold on to the boat railings a little bit longer. If you personally choose to come near to Him, He promises not only to hold your hand but to draw near to you and dance out each and every dream you have, all while laughing in great joy during your time spent together.

Where do you find yourself regarding your dreams and desires? Are you frustrated, as they lie in a coma? Do you find yourself clinging to the comforts of the boat? Uncomfortable with the idea of stepping out? Are you asking God, like Nacho and myself, "Precious Father, why did you give me these desires in the first place, but made me such a stinky _____ (insert your dream here)"?

There is something very special about living out our dreams together with Him. Are you ready to take His hand and walk into the unknown? If so, it will require letting go—letting go of the boat, letting go your timing, and letting go of your dreams altogether.

Reflection Questions:

What are your dreams and desires? When did these desires enter your heart?

Label the approximate time you began to have these dreams and desires for your

life.

_____

_____

_____

_____

_____

_____

_____

_____

_____

_____

_____

Have you seen some of them come to fruition yet? If so, write about how they came together. Include every God-orchestrated detail involved while you praise and honor Him for bringing them to life.

_____

_____

_____

_____

_____

_____

_____

_____

_____

_____

_____

Are there certain dreams and desires that have not taken flight yet? If so, which ones? And why do you think they have not come true yet?

_____

_____

_____

_____

_____

_____

_____

_____

_____

_____

_____

Spend some time in worship, thanking Him for all that He has placed inside you.

Take this time to surrender your dreams and desires back to Him. Let go of the

idea that it is up to you to make them happen, and just lay them surrendered at His

feet. A heart of worship and surrender reveals a willing heart for God to work through. Listen closely, He has some things to share with you during this special time with Him.

As you worship Him with a grateful heart, what are you experiencing? How would you describe His presence? What is He saying to you?

_____

_____

_____

_____

_____

_____

_____

_____

_____

_____

_____

_____

Write down all that He is personally downloading in you regarding your dreams and desires. As you do, you can rest in knowing each one of them is in good, good hands with Him.

_____

_____

_____

_____

_____

_____

_____

_____

_____

_____

_____

_____

You may see yourself as a stinky warrior, but He sees your God-size dreams and desires. He is the One who has placed them in the depths of your heart in the first place. His desire is to dance them out with you, as you both laugh over stormy seas—*together*.

CHAPTER 6

See You Tomorrow

Most nights before bed, my husband, Joe, and I would tuck our daughter Sofia in with a devotion, a prayer, three encouragements for each other, plus a big ole hug and a kiss. As we left her room, Sof would naturally shout out, "See you tomorrow!" with sincere confidence, joy, and the knowledge she would see us tomorrow and we would do this all over again.

It turned into a game in our family, as to who could say it in the final moments as we all raced to bed. Joe and I would laugh as we tried to get the last word in as the door shut quickly behind us. Then, echoing from the bedroom walls, we could hear Sof yell out in the final round, "SEE YOU TOMORROW!" And we would all laugh.

This would go on and on, back and forth, until we would all fall asleep, when all along it had nothing to do with tomorrow but everything to do with the joy we were having today. It became a regular evening routine, as she grew from a toddler to a teenager, and even now, as she attends her first year of college, we hang up the phone with "See you tomorrow!"

There is a promise I love in God's Word that reminds me about tomorrow. It is found in Matthew 6:25–34 (ERV):

"So I tell you, don't worry about the things you need to live—what you will eat, drink, or wear. Life is more important than food, and the body is more important than what you put on it. Look at the birds. They don't plant, harvest, or save food in barns, but your heavenly Father feeds them. Don't you know you are worth much more than they are? You cannot add any time to your life by worrying about it."

"And why do you worry about clothes? Look at the wildflowers in the field. See how they grow. They don't work or make clothes for themselves. But I tell you that even Solomon, the great and rich king, was not dressed as beautifully as one of these flowers. If God makes what grows in the field so beautiful, what do you think he will do for you? It's just grass—one day it's alive, and the next day someone throws it into a fire. But God cares enough to make it beautiful. Surely he will do much more for you. Your faith is so small!"

"Don't worry and say, 'What will we eat?' or 'What will we drink?' or 'What will we wear?' That's what those people who don't know God are always thinking about. Don't worry, because your Father in heaven knows that you need all these things. What you should want most is God's kingdom and doing what he wants you to do. Then he will give you all these other things you need. So don't worry about tomorrow. Each day has enough trouble of its own. Tomorrow will have its own worries."

I have always lived my life with a plan; I am a planner, that is what I do: I plan. Tomorrow has always had a plan, along with the next day, the next week, the next month, and even the next year. But I find myself, right now, today, restless and, as weird as it sounds, without a plan.

Letting go of your own will, will always place you in a position of having to let go of your own plan. It will cause your flesh to crawl like the zombies' cry at night in the movie *I Am Legend.* It will get you to question your perspective, your faith, and your trust in God because your physical being craves the busyness of life and the *need* for a plan, while your spirit grows in the quietness of resting in Him.

It confronts this idea that your occupation is your identity or what you do in life is what gives you value: the people you know, the title you have, the things you call your own. It is a position of letting it all hang out before God, vulnerable and naked before Him. Stripped completely from the security of an agenda because you know you have no control. That is where I find myself, that is where I'm at, wanting to plan my tomorrow but unable to do so.

Thank God for Job. I don't know if you've read his story, but if you haven't yet, you should. It will make you feel a million times better about your own life. The man lost it all, within a few days—well, almost everything. He still had his bad-attitude wife (which I have a feeling, he kind of wished she would have been swept away with the house, but that is just my opinion). In his loss he had to learn to let go and rather quickly.

In Job's own words, but with a rock-star God attitude, he stated, "When I was born into this world, I was naked and had nothing. When I die and leave this world, I will be naked and have nothing. The Lord gives, and the Lord takes away. Praise the name of the Lord" (Job 1:21 ERV). Seriously! Thank God for Job!

Then we see his health compromised while his besties come over and question his integrity. (Ouch!!!) The man's got nothing good left. He has been stripped of his family, reputation, livelihood, and health with a revelation of his new reality, terrible friends, and a nagging wife. We start to see Job's flesh crawl like the zombies in *I Am Legend* as we read chapter 3; Job curses the day he was born. Again, thank God for Job. He's not perfect, he's just straight-up real with his frustrations, questioning his situation of today so he can plan out his tomorrow (I'm sure of it). Who could blame him?!

As Job's friends point fingers at his current condition, we find Job trying to make sense of his situation. Their conversations continue through chapter 37, back and forth, on and on, until God chimes in. You may want to start here, Job 38; this is where it gets good and quite humorous.

By the way, I have what I like to call a heavenly imagination, so when I spend time reading God's Word, I try to picture myself there, in that moment, and sometimes, well, it gets pretty inventive, so bear with me. It's as if God has been *patiently* listening to the back-and-forth banter between Job and his pals, until He can't listen anymore. I picture God rolling His eyes in mild annoyance, like moms do when they overhear their kids quarrelling about the ownership of their toys— "No, it's mine!" "NO, it's NOT, it's MINE!!!"—when all along, *really*, the gosh-darn toys are moms, because she's the one who bought them in the first place!

God begins to question Job with questions only God Almighty can ask (and answer). "Where were you when I made the earth? If you are so smart, answer me" (Job 38:4 ERV). Boom! Roasted. And the questions just keep rolling. Every detailed question could turn an atheist into a born-again believer in a matter of seconds.

But it seems necessary for God to ask such things. Job was wrestling through this situation with his own understanding. He had no way of truly comprehending what was really taking place behind the scenes. If we jump back to Job 1, we can see why this really happened in the first place; it may appear to us that Job was completely blindfolded and sideswiped and left in the dark, but *really*, God recognized Job as a good man. God apparently trusted Job, because He is the one who orchestrated the letting go in the first place.

As we read Job's almost speechless response to God in chapter 40 (after the mic drop of straightforward questioning), Job's repentance and admiration reveal why God had His eye on Job from the very beginning. Job recognized God as God. Period. His losses could not change that. His friends could not sway him. His wife could not convince him otherwise.

There is a lot we can learn in our losses too. When we find ourselves having to answer the question honestly, do we *truly* believe that God is God?

Even in the moments when things do not seem fair but are necessary in understanding who He is? When the plans of tomorrow seem to reveal no plans at all? When the question marks of uncertainty lead us along like all the what-ifs we find in Matthew 6? When God *patiently* listens to us while we try to figure it all out on our own, all along, behind the scenes, He sees it all and He knows it all.

His sovereignty reminds us there is way more to this than we can possibly understand, comprehend, or make sense of. In these moments, God is whispering (can you hear Him?), "The story's not over yet. Hang on. We will deal with tomorrow, tomorrow. For now, trust who I Am and trust Me with today. I'm working all things out for *your good*."

Speaking of stories, back to Job. Good news! God restores him. (One more time, say it with me: thank God for Job!) His restoration included terms such as *again, much,* and *more*! God restored Job's life and livelihood; He took care of his tomorrow while remaining the same God of today.

I guess I will put it bluntly to you, like Jesus does in His Word for me: don't worry. I know that sounds easier said than done, but His Word states it nonetheless. Your Father in heaven knows exactly what you need—today, tomorrow, the next day, next week, and even ten years from now. He reminds us of this promise as we look at His creation, when we take a walk in nature, when we listen to His whisper; He shares it in His Word; we can find it in His presence and even in our hope-filled plans (or lack thereof). He is in the details of our every day, period—even when we feel blindfolded, sideswiped, and left in the dark.

Reflection Questions:

Let's be real. What plans or ideas for tomorrow have you had that seem to be

nonexistent now?

_____

_____

_____

_____

_____

_____

_____

_____

_____

_____

_____

_____

What is responsible for your feelings of uncertainty when it comes to tomorrow

(fear, doubt, lack, insecurity, circumstances, etc.)?

_____

_____

_____

_____

_____

_____

_____

_____

_____

_____

_____

_____

What worries keep surfacing and why? Write it all down, even if your writing

turns to scribbles of frustration. God can handle it.

_____

_____

_____

_____

_____

_____

_____

_____

_____

_____

_____

_____

_____

When you feel like you have gotten it all out on paper, turn to Job 38:1 and read it

all the way through to Job 41:34. As you read God's questions to Job *out loud,*

make them personal for you. Sip your coffee or drink your tea while He asks you

some honest and real truths; then try to answer them, if you think you can.

As you finish reading, what does this leave you believing about God—who He is,

what He's done, and what He can do?

_____

_____

_____

_____

_____

_____

_____

_____

_____

_____

_____

_____

How does understanding and knowing His greatness impact you, your

circumstance, your situation, your lack, and your loss?

_____

_____

_____

_____

_____

_____

_____

_____

_____

_____

_____

_____

_____

Is there possibly something happening behind the scenes that you may not understand but He knows everything about?

_____

_____

_____

_____

_____

_____

_____

_____

_____

_____

_____

_____

_____

How does recognizing God as God change the way you see tomorrow? Your

plans? Your ideas?

_____

_____

_____

_____

_____

_____

_____

_____

_____

_____

_____

_____

What can you praise Him for, as Job did (Job 1:21), even through your hits, your

losses, and your letting go? Write it all down, as a thank-you letter of worship to

Him.

_____

_____

_____

_____

_____

_____

_____

_____

_____

You may have been questioning and wondering if you will see Him tomorrow and that's okay. I think we all do. But just remember, it is His promise to you. Don't worry, He has got it covered. Listen as He shouts, in the final round before bed, "SEE YOU TOMORROW!"—with sincere confidence, joy, and the knowledge He plans to do this each day with you.

CHAPTER 7

Be Still

You can learn a lot about yourself and God in the stillness. I think, to a degree, we all encountered some stillness during the beginning months of quarantine. Everything shut down, the pace of life changed, and we were all forced to just be still. Did you feel stir-crazy? I know I did. Stillness can be boring, uncomfortable, frustrating, and irritating. At least that is what I always thought. But some of the greatest lessons I have learned about myself, and God, I have found in the stillness.

I will admit, I am a Martha more than a Mary. I am a doer. A busybody. Always on the move with lists upon lists upon lists of things to complete. Nothing seems more satisfying than crossing off a completed to-do item from my list (ah, satisfaction!), and then I am on to the next thing. So being still is not a natural action for me, by any means.

The word *still*, as a verb, is defined by Merriam-Webster as "to become motionless or silent: QUIET."[3] I define the verb *still* in this study because I am learning how vital it is that we are intentional in taking the action to be still as a part of our everyday lives with Him.

In January of 2019 I was confronted with the need to be still. I was

exhausted, drained, worn-out, burned-out, and spent. I began to recognize that I

had stretched myself too thin over the previous six months with doing more,

taking on more, and filling my schedule with more. (Have you been there?!) The

mental, spiritual, and emotional anguish I endured during that season felt

exhausting and suffocating.

I felt like I could not keep my head above water to catch my breath quick

enough. It was a painful season for me where I felt completely depleted. It was as

if I was clinging to the baby toe of Jesus with a two-finger grip, about to slip

deeper and deeper into this sea of despair. I found myself paralyzed emotionally,

physically, spiritually, and mentally while I felt God whispering to me, "Be still"

(Psalm 46:10 NLT).

It is amazing what you will learn about yourself and God in the stillness.

God began to reveal my unhealthy reliance on people, my focus on what is *not*

important, and the time wasted on wasteful activities. As humbling and

challenging this was to learn about myself, it was also incredibly freeing. As I

surrendered, He gently reinforced that He is my *One* and my *only*. My rock,

refuge, and strength.

God began to teach me the goodness of letting go. He was cleaning up the toxic relationships I clung to and absolving bad habits that I did not even know I had. He began to prepare me for future seasons of letting go, while He reminded me, it is all a part of this faith journey we have with Him.

In those moments of being intentionally still with Him, I encountered more of Jesus and His presence than ever before, more than any event I had led, any worship service I had gone to, or any program I was a part of. He began to revitalize every detail of the turmoil I was encountering and filling me with His rest, His presence, His healing, His joy, His hope, and His peace. It became my morning routine and my daily mantra just to *be still* with Him.

In 1 Kings 19:11–12 (GW), God told Elijah, "'Go out and stand in front of the LORD on the mountain.' As the LORD was passing by, a fierce wind tore mountains and shattered rocks ahead of the LORD. But the LORD was not in the wind. After the wind came an earthquake. But the LORD wasn't in the earthquake. After the earthquake there was a fire. But the LORD wasn't in the fire. And after the fire there was a quiet, whispering voice."

If you do not know the behind-the-scenes story of Elijah, you *need* to check it out. Elijah was a *rock-star* man of faith. God used him mightily. He was well-known in his time throughout the land; chapter after chapter in 1 Kings prove it! Miracle after miracle, event after event, God showed up and moved in Elijah's life.

Right before this whisper encounter in 1 Kings 19, Elijah and God teamed up against 450 prophets of Baal for what I like to call a bonfire-off, found in 1 Kings 18. Basically, the bonfire-off consisted of determining whose god, the God of Israel versus the god of Baal, could fire up the sacrificial fire pit without any human striking a match—this would prove *who* the real true God was. (Don't you wish you could have been there with s'mores in tow?!) Our boy, Elijah, gave the Baal peeps the first go.

In 1 Kings 18, you can see the Baal worshippers *going off* from morning till evening: they prayed, they danced, they shouted, they cut themselves, blood spewing, dripping, and gushing. They did *everything* they could to get Baal's attention, but Baal did not seem to be available. Elijah began to make fun of them and say things like, "Maybe you should shout louder so he can hear you!" Elijah begins to laugh and make jokes that maybe Baal is using the bathroom (and cannot get to the phone right now! Please leave a message at the beep!). PS. Elijah's a funny guy! It did not matter how loud, how reckless, how crazy they were or how much blood they lost—Baal was unavailable and unresponsive.

It was Elijah's turn. He took twelve stones to rebuild the altar, he sent servants to pour water over the altar three times, until the water was flowing like the Mississippi river. He prayed a simple prayer to God and *shazam*! Fire consumed the entire altar, like the *best* bonfire you have ever gone to on a fall, crisp evening with a group of your bestest friends. The people began to bow down and chant over and over again, "The Lord is God" (1 Kings 18:39 ERV). Elijah then slaughtered each and every prophet of Baal as they tried to run away. Pretty stinkin' sweet, huh?!

So, why do we find Elijah not too long after this incredible God-powerful event frightened and running for his life? First Kings 19 tells us that he ran into the wilderness, he sits under a tree, and he wants to die. He is exhausted, drained, worn-out, burnt-out, and spent. It is from there God leads him to His stillness, His whisper. Obviously, God is in *all* the details of life. We see those details clearly, front and center in Elijah's life. The big miracles, the goosebump moments, the exciting blessings.

Those big, loud moments seem to mesmerize us; they get us on a spiritual high, and we end up trying to live off these encounters to keep us engaged and oftentimes entertained. But I wonder what would happen if we looked for Him more often in the little ones, the unimportant parts of our day, the simple and the quiet. You know, the mundane, boring, chill and still moments—before the alarm goes off, the kids wake up, the news goes on, and the phone lights up.

Whether you believe this or not, I have personally come to the place of recognizing that stillness in His presence is a superpower. It is a time when He refreshes our soul, invigorates our body, clears our mind, simmers our emotions, and centers our attention exactly where it is supposed to be: on Him and Him alone. Our activities cannot do this, our events (even if they are church related) cannot fully provide it, our screen time will not allow for it. It is only in our stillness with Him that we can fully hear the depth of His whisper that fills us up to overflowing.

Elijah, the man of God who was cool enough to make it in the best-selling book of all time, had to learn this, just as I, a regular chick from the Midwest, had to learn it too. What about you? Have you discovered this stillness with Him? Are you in a season like I was or Elijah was, feeling consumed by busyness, exhausted by events, involved in constant activity, people needing something from you at every turn? Emotionally drained, physically exhausted, burnt-out by life and desperate for revitalization?

Being still for you might mean stop talking. Quit trying to figure it all out. Stop fighting. Quit looking for answers in places that you won't find *the* answer.

Put an end to thinking you are in control. Terminate the idea that your busyness equals fruitfulness. Halt the notion that your voice must be heard. Cease the overthinking, the overdoing, the constant rhetoric in your thoughts and elsewhere. And just be still and know that He is God.

Is God trying to encourage you in His stillness? I dare you to try it. His whisper may be faint because He knows you must lean in to hear it. To quiet yourself and your surroundings. To disengage from the distractions and to just . . . be still.

Shut yourself in a quiet room. No phone, no people, no TV, no distractions. Leave your cares, worries, and thoughts on paper somewhere else and just close the door.

As you try it, how do you feel? What is racing through your mind? What is your flesh craving? Why does it feel so hard to be still?

I encourage you to do this every single day for one week. Make it a priority in your schedule, just like you would a shower, your school work, a job, eating, brushing your teeth, or anything else that is vital for you to complete in a day. Give God the beginning of your day, to be still in His presence; there is something powerful and beautiful about putting Him first. Your flesh will get antsy, your mind will begin to race, your A.D.D. will kick in, but it's okay, just

continue to BE STILL.

Reflection Questions:

After a week of being still with Him, what did He reveal to you?

_____

_____

_____

_____

_____

_____

_____

_____

_____

_____

_____

What areas in your life does He need to take priority over?

_____

_____

_____

_____

_____

_____

_____

_____

_____

_____

_____

Describe what happened in you from the first day of being still to the last day.

_____

_____

_____

_____

_____

_____

_____

_____

_____

_____

_____

_____

What words, pictures, visions, or ideas did He give you during these moments?

Write each of them down, regardless of whether or not it makes sense right now.

_____

_____

_____

_____

_____

_____

_____

_____

_____

_____

_____

_____

How has the action of being still in His presence for one week impacted you?

_____

_____

_____

_____

_____

_____

_____

_____

_____

_____

_____

Is this something you will continue to do, making it a part of your everyday

routine? Why or why not?

_____

_____

_____

_____

_____

_____

_____

_____

_____

_____

How has the stillness allowed you to hear His whisper more clearly?

_____

_____

_____

_____

_____

_____

_____

_____

_____

_____

_____

How has being still allowed His whisper to become the loudest voice throughout your day?

_____

_____

_____

_____

_____

_____

_____

_____

_____

_____

_____

_____

_____

You can learn a lot about yourself and God in the stillness.

CHAPTER 8

New

New . . . it has an exciting, refreshing, joyful ring to it, doesn't it? We love the idea of *new*. It gives us butterflies and excitement. It provides us with content for our Instagram, creates updates for our followers on Facebook, and allows for fun conversations over coffee with friends. I've been learning a whole lot about the *new* God has for us through this journey of letting go, have you? The *new* will always require a not-so-glamorous season of letting go.

In 2005 I graduated from college as a single mom with three jobs. I worked hard and I was excited about this accomplishment as I planned to begin my new career, with Jesus leading the way. I obtained my bachelor of science degree in therapeutic recreation with one goal in mind: to change the world! (I hear you laughing at my naivete). I was a new graduate with *big* dreams and a *huge* passion to help others, specifically kids, encounter hope, joy, and fun in their journey. It was my mission, my purpose, and the world was my oyster! (Again, I can hear you!)

As my job search began, my resume went out, screaming my potential and shouting my skill set, like a politician the day before an election. My new dream job was almost within my grasp, I could feel it; with every application, my heart yelled, "Pick me! Pick me!" But as the months went by, the job search ran longer than expected.

The process challenged my mission and my purpose, leaving me with questions and a whole lot of confusion. Did I waste all those years pursuing a college degree for a career I was not called to? Why so many closed doors? Did I miss You, God? Did I miss . . . *something*? My goal to change the world conflicted with my reality, while the strain of the waiting season began to weigh down my hope.

I felt embarrassed, unsuccessful, with no future in sight. And being a single mom in my late twenties didn't help. I strained and strived, trying to find the open door, but I sensed God was actively confronting my pride, challenging my vanity, and questioning my source.

The months turned into years (two years to be exact) of this in-between season of seeking God in surrender while I tried to understand His will for my life. In the meantime I began my own cleaning business while I waited, hanging on to hope by a thread, for my exciting new career to begin in rec therapy. The process of every closed door kept me clinging to Jesus, not fully understanding what He was up to but recognizing He was shutting doors to prepare me for something *new*.

I was done having my way. I had already seen the results of *me* taking control in the past, so with every day that went by, I surrendered my plan to receive His. I began to let go of rec therapy, to let go of my agenda and fully commit to whatever He was leading me to.

Don't get me wrong, the process was painful and challenging, frustrating and irritating. I had to intentionally let go of my will every day as my tantrum of control made me want to burst (please tell me you have been there). I cried a lot as I laid my vision, my aspiration, my college degree, and my future career at the feet of the *One* whom I knew (that I knew, that I knew) I could trust.

As I laid it all down, I began to see more clearly what He was up to. He was working on something new behind the scenes, even while I cried and threw tantrums like a toddler. He was up to something good that was stretching my faith and causing me to wait patiently on Him.

In 2007 the door swung wide open to something new; to lead the children's program at my church, voluntarily. My heart screamed with excitement while my skills and abilities in ministry lacked confidence, experience, and talent.

Yet my church took a big ole leap of faith and allowed me to step into the role as the children's pastor.

As I stepped out, I held His hand and watched Him navigate my dreams, my mission, and my passion (which He gave me in the first place, mind you) to help others, specifically *these* kids, encounter hope, joy, and fun in their faith journey. It was not how I planned it, but how He had.

What began as a step of faith turned into thirteen years of ministry with Him molding my trust in Him, defining my identity, and allowing me to be His vessel for the calling He placed on my life. Something I could only encounter as I let go. I'm forever grateful for that two-year season of the in-between, not-so-glamourous, painful, troubling, and challenging time of letting go; it was exactly where I found freedom in surrender and experienced His new plan for me.

James 1:2–4 (NLT) encourages us, "Dear brothers and sisters,[a] when troubles of any kind come your way, consider it an opportunity for great joy. For you know that when your faith is tested, your endurance has a chance to grow. So let it grow, for when your endurance is fully developed, you will be perfect and complete, needing nothing."

By the way, thank you for joining me on this journey, I am glad to know I am not the only one. By now, I'm sure you've already felt the in-between-waiting and refining, the crushing, the pressing, and the darn right pain of letting go—letting go of your own dreams, situations, heartache, comforts, people, opinions, plans, hatred (and *everything* else in-between)! You've journaled through these pages with honesty and sincerity; you've bared your soul and let it all hang out before Him. Thanks again for going on this wild ride with me.

The good news is, it's not just us—there are others too, plenty more. We can find them throughout the pages of His Word, the not-so-glamorous journey of others having to let go as well. Take the Israelites, for instance, as they left Egypt in the book of Numbers.

Their excitement for the *new* (the Promised Land) but the reality of a forty-year journey that should have only taken eleven days was all a part of the letting-go process. Fear, disobedience, and rebellion can slow our journey down, but it is good to know that God is so *patient* with us, right?! Their familiar past in Egypt seemed to lure them back a few too many times. It took a while, but they finally got there; maybe it has taken you a while too, but it's okay, He's still walking with you, holding your hand. He has got something *new* just for you as well.

Remember in the Gospels when Jesus called Matthew to follow Him? Matthew had to give up his ways, his job, and even his high-end lifestyle for a *new* life with Him. I'm sure his mind twitched with the thought of losing it all, but Matthew knew there was much more to his story, as he counted the cost of letting go of the old to receive the *new*.

What about the sinful and scandalous woman in Luke 7, when she just showed up (*uninvited*!) to a house filled with "important" people. Her reasons: to shower her love and gratitude for Jesus, by washing His feet and anointing His head with expensive perfume in front of *everyone*! She had a lot to lose: her reputation, her past, and any people-pleasing (she may have had before) to walk into that place, as men stared her down in judgment. But she didn't seem to care; she walked in with her full attention on the *One* who could bring her a *new* identity, a *new* calling, and a *new* purpose, never batting an eye to what any of them had to say about her. Her *new* in Him was worth letting go of everything.

And. Oh. My. Goodness! Have you checked out Paul's life in the book of Acts?! He went from murderer to missionary in a matter of days. The process of letting go included God removing the scales from his eyes for him to *truly* see and step into his new beginning with Christ. Paul was blind for three whole days; he did not eat or drink. Can you imagine his process of letting go?! (Ughhh!) I can only envision what battled in his thoughts and emotions over those few days, the guilt that clamored for his attention, the shame that tried to steal his new mission, and the lies that tried to creep in and remind him of who he used to be. But Jesus had *new* plans and a *new* call for Paul; He redefined his identity, renewed his story, and refreshed his soul. Paul was now a *new* man.

A *new* perspective requires letting go of opinions. A *new* heart requires letting go of the past. A *new* dream requires letting go of unnecessary desires. A *new* outcome requires letting go of bad habits. And a *new* life requires letting go of what was. Hopefully, it's becoming more clear: the *new* in Him will always require letting go of something and that something is always worth letting go of.

There is a song called "New Wine" by Hillsong Worship; have you heard it? If you have not, I encourage you to listen to it on your journey of letting go. It has become one of my favorites. Its lyrics speak of this great exchange He offers us. The crushing and the pressing during the letting-go moments, but the new that comes forth with this exchange. Its melody sings of the surrender involved— giving up our soil so He can break new ground and bring about His new foundation in us. The words remind us as we yield to Him and trust Him alone; we do not need to fully understand all the details, but just to trust- He is in control. The words prompt us and affirm us—when we come to Him, we have absolutely nothing but what He has already given us, allowing Him to make us whatever He wants us to be.

This letting go gives way for the *new* He has for us. *New* freedom, *new* power, *new* fire, *new* understanding, *new* gifts, *new* purpose, *new* life, and all the *new* our souls can handle. What *new* are you experiencing in Him as you are letting go?

Reflection Questions:

We have been on a journey, of letting go, together. Thanks again for joining me.

As we close out this devotional, consider the cost you have made for letting go.

Write down what you have given up over the course of our journey together—

your comfort, your opinions, your dreams, your plans, your way, your control.

Have you had to let go of hatred, anger, or bitterness that you had every right to

have? How about your way of seeing things? Your plans for tomorrow? Your

ideas? Your old life? Your habits? Perfection? People-pleasing? Write it all here.

_____

_____

_____

_____

_____

_____

_____

_____

_____

_____

_____

_____

As you have been letting go, how has it felt, honestly?

_____

_____

_____

_____

_____

_____

_____

_____

_____

_____

What has this process confronted in you?

_____

_____

_____

_____

_____

_____

_____

_____

_____

_____

_____

What have been your greatest challenges through this letting-go journey?

_____

_____

_____

_____

What freedoms have you found in surrender?

_____

_____

_____

_____

_____

What "*new*" has Jesus been filling you with? Fill this space with the *new* He's

doing in you.

_____

_____

_____

_____

_____

_____

_____

_____

_____

_____

_____

I want to leave you with some encouragement—God's promises of the *new* He

has just for you. Hold onto them tightly, with a faith-filled grip. They are His

words and His gifts as He reminds you of His goodness, grace, and generosity in

this journey of letting go.

- Isaiah 43:18–19 (ERV) says, "So don't remember what happened in earlier times. Don't think about what happened a long time ago, because I am doing something new! Now you will grow like a new plant. Surely you know this is true. I will even make a road in the desert, and rivers will flow through that dry land."

- Second Corinthians 5:17 (NLT) says, "This means that anyone who belongs to Christ has become a new person. The old life is gone; a new life has begun!"

- Ephesians 2:10 (ERV) says, "God has made us what we are. In Christ Jesus, God made us new people so that we would spend our lives doing the good things he had already planned for us to do."

- Ezekiel 36:26 (GW) says, "I will give you a new heart and put a new spirit in you. I will remove your stubborn hearts and give you obedient hearts."

- Isaiah 40:31 (NLT) says, "But those who trust in the LORD will find new strength. They will soar high on wings like eagles. They will run and not grow weary. They will walk and not faint."

- Revelation 21:5 (NLT) says, "And the one sitting on the throne said, 'Look, I am making everything new!' And then he said to me, 'Write this down, for what I tell you is trustworthy and true.'"

CONCLUSION

As we say good-bye, I hope and pray that you have encountered the power, love, and presence of Jesus through the pages of this devotional. I know some of the soul-searching and digging deep can be difficult to rehash and walk through, but I am believing with you that you will experience all that God promises in His Word just for you, in your season of letting go. That you will find freedom in surrender and experience the goodness of God—His restoration, healing, peace, and all the newness your soul can handle.

I hope my stories have encouraged you, made you laugh, or even helped you to see that you are not alone in this journey. Anytime you find yourself in another season of having to let go, please meet me back here and we will do it all over again—together. As we close, I want to leave you with these beautiful words from James 1:17–18 (ERV) to meditate on and rest in, knowing that you are His most treasured and He values you:

"Everything good comes from God. Every perfect gift is from him. These good gifts come down from the Father who made all the lights in the sky. But God never changes like the shadows from those lights. He is always the same.

God decided to give us life through the true message he sent to us. He wanted us to be the most important of all that he created."

Much love and sincerity,

Jodi

ACKNOWLEDGMENTS

Inspiration can be found anywhere, especially when we look for it. I've been finding my inspiration over the years in people I spend time with, in nature walks, in His Word, through music, in books I'm reading, and in times of being still with God, giving me the joy and the courage to step out and create this dear-to-my-heart devotional and journal.

I want first to give credit where credit is due. Thank You, Jesus, for doing life with me. For leading me and loving me exactly where I am, always. You downloaded every detail of this devotional into the depths of my heart for such a time as this. Thank you for teaching me the goodness of letting go, as I share this personal journey to encourage others.

Joe and Sof—Thank you for your constant love and encouragement. Thank you for being my cheering section in life. The gifts God has placed in both of you encourages and inspires me to use mine; your boldness and willingness to step out motivates me to do the same. I love you two with all my heart.

Mom and Dad—Thank you for your constant love and support, always reminding me, "God broke the mold when He made you." You two are some of the most generous, merciful, and compassionate people I have ever known. Thank you for letting me read to you and for being a beautiful example of Jesus to our entire family. I love you both so very much!

My sibs—I love you guys! Thank you for letting me talk about our crazy childhood in the pages of this book! Greg, your humor makes the world a better place! Thank you for always bringing joy to every situation; you never fail to light up a room and bring laughter to my life. Forever Biggie. Jen, not a day goes by where I don't hear from you (it must be your number two personality!). Thank you for always being there for me, whether we are chatting, crying, laughing, or growling over texts, DMs, video chats, calls, or now in-person visits. Either way, I appreciate our kinship more than you will ever know. Leah, your creativity and perseverance amaze me. You reflect your God gifts so beautifully and intentionally while inspiring others to do the same. Thank you for teaching me how to take this next step. You will always be my Ely Eleanora!

The Victory Kids (Ann Arbor Assembly of God)—The thirteen years of growing in faith with you were some of the best years of my life! Thank you for your patience with me while I stepped out in crazy faith as a minister and for allowing me to be my crazy self, always. You provided me the opportunity and grace to grow, as I wrote the Victory Kid curriculum and the Remix devotionals. You gave me the chance to speak, teach, and lead creatively, comically, and interactively, and it was an absolute blast! Learning about Jesus with each one of *you* and growing in our faith *together* has been a beautiful blessing! Our times of laughter, praise, worship, and God's presence have forever molded who I am today. Please tell John I said hi! I miss each one of you so very much. Keep your eyes *fixed* on Jesus; He has some amazing and exciting plans prepared just for *you*!

My Michigan friends—Thank you for your friendship! Our numerous coffee dates, walks, chats, bonfires, and Coney Island breakfasts are forever engraved in my heart. The time spent with each one of you (for sometimes hours at a time) encouraged my soul and refreshed my spirit immensely. Thank you for being the real deal and for doing life with me. I am forever and always grateful for our laughs, our cries, and our times of everything in between. Your friendship is gold and has meant the world to me. Our friendship continues, even from afar.

Deb Hall—My editor. You are the best! Thank you for your patience, flexibility, help, generosity, thoughtfulness, and willingness to teach me and assist me through this manuscript. What a magnificent editor and teacher you are. I appreciate *you*!

Lastly, to those who don't know me but have inspired me through their teachings and writings (Sarah Young, Bob Goff, Joyce Meyer, Shawn Bolz,

Steven Furtick, Amanda Pittman, Dr. Tony Evans, Morgan Harper Nichols, Michael and Jess Koulianos, Havilah Cunnington, Dutch Sheets, Bobby Gruenewald and Craig Groeschel)—Thank you! Your words through books, social media, preaching, teaching, and devotionals inspire numerous people to follow Jesus and understand His extravagant love for them. You lead and encourage others with God's authenticity, kindness, and truth. Thank you for doing this for me; I am one of many who are grateful. Your encouraging words have inspired my faith journey to new dreams and new places.

NOTES

1. "Binding," *Yourdictionary.com*, accessed November 5, 2020, https://www.yourdictionary.com/binding.

2. *Nacho Libre*, directed by Jared Hess (2006; Oaxaca, Mexico: Paramount Pictures, 2006), DVD.

3. "Still," *Merriam-Webster.com Dictionary*, accessed November 5, 2020, https://www.merriam-webster.com/dictionary/still.

Made in the USA
Columbia, SC
10 December 2020